Mythical Mermaids Mosaic Color by Number Coloring Book for Adults Enchanted Fantasy Women Under the Ocean For Stress Relief and Relaxation

By Color Questopia

Thank you
for your purchase!

**Claim your FREE digital copy of our
Highlight Reel Color By Number Book:**

Check out our website: colorquestopia.com

**Join our Facebook group:
facebook.com/colorquestopia**

Follow us on Instagram: @colorquestopia

**Did you enjoy this book?
Please leave us a review!**

https://geni.us/cqreview

Color By Number Tips

1. **Relax and have fun**
   Let your cares slip away as you color the images. Take your time. Coloring is a meditative activity and there's no wrong way to do it. Feel free to color as you listen to music, watch TV, lounge in bed- do whatever relaxes you most! You can also color while you're out and about- on the train or at a cafe- take the book with you anywhere you go. Coloring is therapeutic and is great for stress relief and relaxation!

2. **Colors corresponding to each number are shown on the back cover of the book**
   Each number corresponds to a color shown on the back of the book. You can match the color as closely as you like- but feel free to change the color or the shade if you don't have the exact color match- that's totally fine. Although this is a color by number book, it's completely okay to get creative and color the images with whichever colors you like and have. The numbers are there to be a guide and to allow you to color without having to focus your energy on choosing colors.

3. **Choose your coloring tools**
   Everyone has their favorite coloring markers, crayons, pencils, pens- even paints! Feel free to color with any tool that you like! If you choose markers or paints, we recommend putting a blank sheet of paper or cardboard behind each image, so that your colors don't run onto the next image.

1. Violet

2. Orange

3. Red

4. Yellow

5. Green

6. Pink

7. Purple

8. Light Brown

9. Medium Brown

10. Peach

11. Hot Pink

12. Light Blue

13. Medium Blue

14. Blue

15. Sky Blue

16. Baby Blue

1. Light Brown
2. Peach
3. Violet
4. Dark Pink
5. Light Pink
6. Orange
7. Hot Pink
8. Purple
9. Light Violet
10. Dark Yellow
11. Medium Purple
12. Red
13. Light Orange
14. Green
15. Yellow
16. Blue
17. Light Blue

1. White

2. Black

3. Medium Brown

4. Light Brown

5. Light Pink

6. Bright Orange

7. Dark Violet

8. Violet

9. Yellow

10. Red

11. Peach

12. Pink

13. Dark Pink

14. Light Violet

15. Purple

16. Orange

17. Light Blue

1. Red
2. Purple
3. Hot Pink
4. Green
5. Yellow
6. Orange
7. Violet
8. Dark Violet
9. Light Violet
10. Medium Purple
11. Peach
12. Medium Orange
13. Pink
14. Light Pink
15. Dark Blue
16. Brown
17. Blue
18. Light Blue

1. Black
2. Light Pink
3. Light Brown
4. Medium Brown
5. Peach
6. Pink
7. Purple
8. Orange
9. Violet
10. Red
11. Yellow
12. Dark Blue
13. Light Violet
14. Medium Purple
15. Light Orange
16. Hot Pink
17. Medium Blue
18. Light Blue

1. Light Brown

2. Medium Brown

3. Pink

4. Yellow

5. Light Pink

6. Violet

7. Light Violet

8. Purple

9. Medium Purple

10. Peach

11. Light Blue

12. Baby Blue

13. Medium Blue

14. Blue

15. Dark Blue

16. Sky Blue

1. Light Brown
2. Pink
3. Purple
4. Peach
5. Violet
6. Dark Yellow
7. Dark Pink
8. Red
9. Light Orange
10. Orange
11. Army Green
12. Beige
13. Green
14. Dark Violet
15. Dark Blue
16. Light Violet
17. Light Pink
18. Baby Blue

1. Light Brown
2. Light Violet
3. Purple
4. Light Pink
5. Bright Orange
6. Pink
7. Dark Green
8. Light Blue
9. Baby Blue
10. Peach
11. Red
12. Dark Yellow
13. Orange
14. Violet
15. Green
16. Medium Orange
17. Blue

1. Light Brown

2. Bright Orange

3. Violet

4. Purple

5. Yellow

6. Pink

7. Dark Violet

8. Green

9. Orange

10. Peach

11. Light Pink

12. Dark Blue

13. Navy Blue

14. Medium Pink

15. Beige

16. Light Blue

17. Baby Blue

1. Light Brown

2. Bright Orange

3. Pink

4. Purple

5. Light Violet

6. Yellow

7. Violet

8. Orange

9. Green

10. Peach

11. Blue

12. Dark Yellow

13. Dark Blue

14. Light Pink

15. Light Green

16. Light Blue

17. Baby Blue

1. Yellow
2. Red
3. Pink
4. Violet
5. Purple
6. Light Pink
7. Orange
8. Dark Pink
9. Green
10. Peach
11. Medium Purple
12. Dark Yellow
13. Medium Pink
14. Light Violet
15. Light Blue
16. Baby Blue
17. Bright Orange

1. Hot Pink
2. Yellow
3. Dark Yellow
4. Pink
5. Light Violet
6. Purple
7. Dark Violet
8. Red
9. Orange
10. Peach
11. Light Pink
12. Green
13. Medium Pink
14. Bright Orange
15. Light Green
16. Brown
17. Light Blue

1. Light Brown   16. Dark Brown

2. Brown   17. Dark Blue

3. Purple   18. Baby Blue

4. Light Violet   19. White

5. Light Pink

6. Pink

7. Dark Pink

8. Red

9. Green

10. Peach

11. Orange

12. Blue

13. Dark Red

14. Light Blue

15. Medium Brown

1. Light Brown
2. Dark Violet
3. Violet
4. Light Violet
5. Purple
6. Pink
7. Light Pink
8. Medium Orange
9. Medium Purple
10. Peach
11. Bright Orange
12. Navy Blue
13. Medium Pink
14. Dark Violet
15. Dark Yellow
16. Baby Blue
17. Blue
18. Light Blue

1. Light Brown
2. Bright Orange
3. Light Violet
4. Violet
5. Yellow
6. Pink
7. Red
8. Light Pink
9. Green
10. Purple
11. Beige
12. Peach
13. Orange
14. Dark Violet
15. Dark Yellow
16. Blue
17. Light Blue
18. Baby Blue

1. Red
2. Black
3. Pink
4. Light Pink
5. Light Violet
6. Baby Blue
7. Orange
8. Violet
9. Peach
10. Purple
11. Green
12. Dark Green
13. Medium Purple
14. Dark Violet
15. Dark Yellow
16. Yellow
17. Light Blue

1. Light Brown

2. Violet

3. Pink

4. Purple

5. Orange

6. Navy Blue

7. Dark Violet

8. Dark Yellow

9. Medium Purple

10. Peach

11. Green

12. Soft Violet

13. Medium Orange

14. Dark Orange

15. Light Violet

16. Yellow

17. Light Blue

1. Purple
2. Yellow
3. Baby Blue
4. Light Violet
5. Bright Orange
6. Medium Blue
7. Dark Violet
8. Orange
9. Green
10. Peach
11. Violet
12. Dark Yellow
13. Medium Pink
14. Light Pink
15. Red
16. Dark Green
17. Dark Blue

1. Light Brown
2. Peach
3. Pink
4. Yellow
5. Light Violet
6. Violet
7. Purple
8. Orange
9. Medium Orange
10. Brown
11. Medium Brown
12. Dark Yellow
13. Medium Pink
14. Light Pink
15. Medium Purple
16. Green
17. Light Blue

1. Purple
2. Baby Blue
3. Pink
4. Yellow
5. Light Violet
6. Violet
7. Dark Orange
8. Orange
9. Light Green
10. Light Pink
11. Dark Yellow
12. Red
13. Dark Red
14. Dark Blue
15. Medium Orange

16. Peach
17. Light Blue

ENJOY BONUS
IMAGES FROM SOME
OF OUR
OTHER FUN
COLOR BY NUMBER
BOOKS!

FIND ALL OF OUR
BOOKS
ON AMAZON

Beautiful Hummingbirds
Mosaic Color By Number
Coloring Book For Adults

1. Black
2. Blue
3. Dark Brown
4. Army Green
5. Red
6. Light Violet
7. Dark Violet
8. Violet
9. Orange
10. Purple
11. Dark Green
12. Brown
13. Light Brown
14. Yellow
15. Pink
16. Green
17. Sky Blue

Fairy Magic
Color By Number
An Enchanted Mosaic
Coloring Book For Adults

1. Dark Brown
2. Peach
3. Red
4. Dark Red
5. Yellow
6. Violet
7. Orange
8. Light Blue
9. Baby Blue
10. Blue
11. Light Green
12. Green
13. Dark Green
14. Medium Green
15. Pink

16. Neon Green
17. Light Gray

Amazing Dogs
Mosaic Color By Number For Adults
Adult Coloring Book

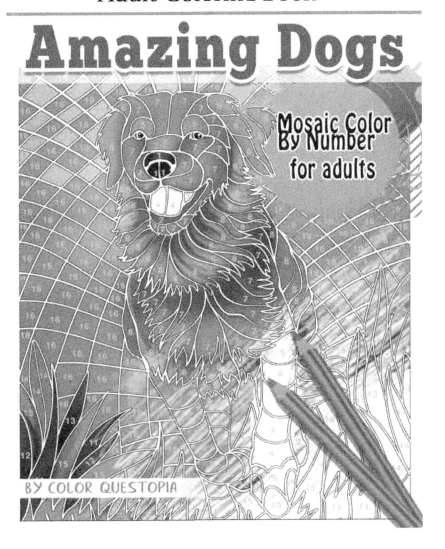

1. Black
2. Hot pink
3. Light yellow
4. Beige
5. Light orange
6. Medium brown
7. Dark yellow
8. Light brown
9. Dark orange
10. Green
11. Army green
12. Medium geen
13. Dark green
14. Light green
15. Sky blue
16. Light pink
17. Baby blue

New York
Mosaic Color by Number
Coloring Book for Adults

1. Red
2. Brown
3. Orange
4. Medium Brown
5. Dark Red
6. Dark Brown
7. Light Violet
8. Gray
9. Light Red
10. Light Orange
11. Light Purple
12. Purple
13. Violet
14. Light Gray
15. Blue
16. Navy Blue
17. Sky Blue

Country Farm Scenes
Nature, Animal, and Easy Designs
Adult Coloring Book
Color By Number For Adults

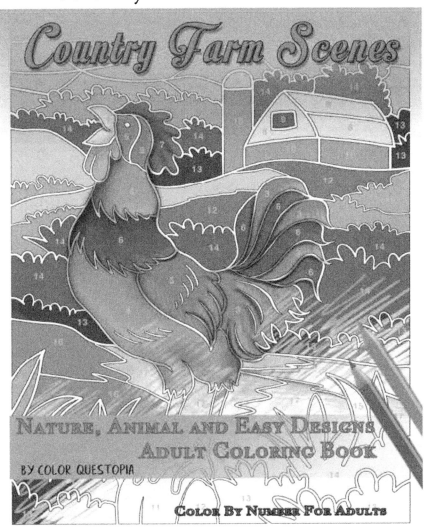

1. Black

2. Pink

3. Dark Brown

4. Brown

5. Medium Brown

6. Dark Green

7. Green

8. Medium Green

9. Light Green

10. Light Brown

11. Light Orange

12. Neon Green

13. Army Green

14. Blue

15. Baby blue

16. Navy Blue

17. Light Blue

Printed in Great Britain
by Amazon

36371325R00040